Gathered at Her Sky

Life Poems by Tantra-zawadi

POETS WEAR PRADA • HOBOKEN, NJ

GATHERED AT HER SKY

First North American Publication 2010.

Copyright © 2010 Tantra-zawadi

Grateful acknowledgment is made to the following individuals and labels who have recorded and produced spoken word tracks on their CDs for some of the poems included here:

Shanna T. Melton (*A Woman's Song*, 2009); Precious Gift (*Selling My Diamonds*, 2000); and Canhead Records (*Urban Avant Garde - Live at the Nuyorican Poet's Café*, 2001).

"Girl" appeared in the print publication *Poetry in Purple* as part of Downstate Medical Center's Domestic Violence Awareness Month in October 2009

ISBN 978-0-9841844-6-0

Printed in the U.S.A.

Front Cover: Photo of Tantra-zawadi by Oliver Covrett; Photo of Lion's Head Mountain in Cape Town, South Africa by Tantra-zawadi Graphic Design by Stephanie Griffin; Cover Concept by Stevie Gee

Back Cover Author Photo: Ansel Pitcairn

*This book is dedicated to Milicent Gaita
and the girls of the Girl Child Network Worldwide.*

The pain is gone!

Preface

Gathered at Her Sky is a fantastic work of poetic humanism, life in poetry, worthy of any coffee table; absolutely soul stirring!

Tantra-Zawadi's poetry speaks of a global consciousness and ambassadorship; each word of every line reminds us of the connection we have to one another in the race to win. The poetry in this collection speaks to the human condition on many levels of existence. This author pays tribute to music's greats, activism, and most importantly of all: Love.

Every home should be furnished with a copy of this chapbook, not just to decorate your living space; to pick up from time to time to let your mind roam across continents, social barriers, and conflict torn lands to in some way give you a sense of belonging to this existence we call "life."

Much like her poetry, Tantra-Zawadi is a humanitarian and a very active actionist on the grind, making people pay attention to what is real in this world; a true ambassador.

Tshombe
Freedom Verse Cafe

Contents

Preface

for eleo pomare   1

A Poem for Haiti   5

For Africa   7

Third Eye Kisses   9

Black Love   13

a poem for jb   17

Girl   19

Secrets   25

Remember Me   27

Girl Blues   29

Acknowledgments

About the Author

for eleo pomare
(1937-2008)

dah, dah, do, do
dah, dah
do, do
dah, dah do
dah dah

flap, ball change
step, step
spin, fly
relevé, jeté
freak it
into first position
pop it

i want to dance

move in the shadows
flex in the light
with collard greens in my teeth
in my bare feet
feel the earth
rumble like bernard and tony
then loving as hard as we could

I've got to dance

move it
swing it
like we used to in the dark
to the horns of dollar cabs
and music in the park

from colombia
to panama
to harlem
i am the energy
the pounding of the boom box
wanna split and hustle
on 125th street
groove with my people
to the ism of malcolm
and the 'ology' of the hip hop beat

dah, dah, do, do
dah, dah
do, do
dah, dah do
dah dah

plié
coupé
with a hand drum

i am sound
ya dig?

made for
black girls with round behinds
and thick thighs

and black boys
who innerstand the risk
But dance anyway
because they've got to

the choreography in my mind
that shifted and molded
r&b 'n hip-hop
'n rosin
developé on the ballet barre
improvise to the inner-size
of my mind
this ain't no dance concert
this is real steps in life

I gotta dance

dah, dah, do, do
dah, dah
do, do
dah, dah do, dah dah

i want to leap
keep time for pomare
you see i am the
contraction
the flex
pointing with my hands
to the sky as the elements
of the universe sing my cries
i fly into the space
especially for me
the floors of the world
birthed on the streets
then pomared into the sets
of our consciousness
I want to dance

dah, dah, do, do
dah, dah
do, do
dah, dah do

can i
can i
just dance
with all that i am
with all that i have
can i
can i
just dance
show you the parts of me
reaching beyond
the parts of me
to a different sound
the hand drum of my soul
the palm print of my solo
on the north side of
125th street

dah, dah do, do
do, dah, dah, do, do

to the steps of real life
the sound of home

dah, dah, do, do
do, dah, dah, do

rest

4

A Poem for Haiti

Toe nails painted red
Fingernails and
Lips thus stained

I look at her cleanly
Parted scalp
with locks of wisdom
and lavender ribbons
Gathered at her sky

Vibrant energy skirted and
Pleated from waist to ankle
With her hands delicately
Placed upon her chest
One on top of the other
Motionless

She was gentle
(I think)
Most likely
Waiting for her groom
for she was a good girl
before she was swallowed

They lay in piles
the brown people tinged gray
and I wonder
if the one with the chocolate hand
was her beloved
Respectfully waiting for his bride

He dreamed of her too
I think
before he was swallowed

Butthereweresomany

Fairies, maidens
Princes, poison apples
and ogres in the agony of
Hushed lullabies and wailing
Absent walls or petitions
Only tears of freedom
Gushing in perfect French
pooling into mud cakes and spirits
that rise from their dust

For Africa

my happy
soles touching
shadeless in her heat
past pimped and stolen
charmed into HIV
diamonds and gold
bleeding forgiveness
restoring her cycle
thick
fragrant
lush
bushy
green sprawling
mines of sacrifice
for africa

cloud topped mountains
shanty towns with tin roofs fired love
praying and chanting
for whom I wonder
as concepts of freedom
consume
the remains of herself
uniting lands
with her blood
her love
the home of her happy
trickled into a fight she did not begin
releasing the shackles of her mind
and her tongue

as the ancestors
remember her happy
shaking her thunder
supportive of her rising
from a war she no longer remembers

(singing)
yeah
yeah
yeah
we are coming together for africa

Third Eye Kisses

Left with the impression of your tribal marks
Where your lips once pressed
Holding on to eternity inside each other/wise
I'd die
If you stopped
Leaving
Impressions of my pillow case
Within my nostrils
The air is somehow changed
And breath comes quicker
Now that I pant to find you
At each and every turning/me/out
You pressed my palm against your mind
So that my beat could become
Your rhythm
My beat could become your rhythm
My beat could become
I sway windward because
I'm so inclined to feel
Blows billowing dreadlocks
Like fires raging
Bright beacons of lighting the way to your love
Scarifications all over my belly from your sizzle
Piercing the smoky aftermath with your arrow
Hitting it each and every time
You leave me no choice
But to lick my own skin colored impressions of you
Solving inches of time
Fused by the fire of my desire
Scattering love like air bound particles of eternity
I mean really
Feeling the length of your desire
Brushing against the thought of my imagination

Equals infinity
Plus
Eternal heat rising passionately so close
That the constellations will cradle our love in light
And we'll praise God for beauty
We'll raise heart in thanksgiving
We mesh minds before thighs
We make love in the way of the spirit
He sun kissed my third eye
I a virgin with full lips
Never been kissed on the mind
Lips locked imagination
Warm honey coursing down my throat
Feeling sweet
Perfect
Still
Sky reaching
Third eye kissed in syncopation with
Spirituality
Discovering my G-spotting
God's most precious gift
Making more sense to kiss me there
Making me come here or wherever
Expansion of higher self is so desired
Or love induced
Cinnamon sugared
Third eye kisses landing squarely
Where I live and think and feel
Praising God for beauty
We'll raise heart in thanksgiving
We mesh minds before thighs
We make love in the way of the spirit
He sun kissed my third eye
I a virgin with full lips
Never been kissed on the mind

Ever so gently he passed through the
Experience of mind pleasure
Like the groove of a Maxwell love song
With sweet pretty poem endings
Cognac laced
Strokes of fingers pointing past
Arias of melodic interest
Kisses tight
Rhythmic verse
From our lips spill a language so sweet
That honey will be our fetish
Next lifetime
And the essence of a Maxwell love song
Will rub our lyrically drenched thoughts
With the will to love deeper than any this
I've never known a man to grant me a third eye kiss
The essence of which alone is enough to raise my
Consciousness
To levels of intoxication
Blowing past the legal limits of feeling
Why do I feel like this?
Humming Bobby Blue Bland sweet notes
When I miss you
I tap/tap my fingers
Sounding out your inner melody
So in tuned to listening
Third eye conscious kissing
He sun kissed my third eye
I a virgin with full lips
Never been kissed
On the mind
His lips pressed my imagination
Wisely seeking the love of me
In places that eyes can't see
I mean really

Feeling the length of your desire
Brushing against the thought
Of my imagination
Equals infinity
Equals infinity
I mean really
Feeling the length of your desire
Brushing against the thought
Of my imagination
Equals infinity

Black Love

ancient
real life
gritty
the color of night
alive
indulged in moonlight
the silver haired
golden continuity of
uniquely committed
unconditionally grounded
the hot comb and whip of civilization
the endless fountain of the all in all

a love poem
it is breathing the same air
walking on the sand
having shoes
rhythm and soul
straight tribal
epic, powerful and tender
the original man and woman
the test of time
wheatgrass and honey
meat and potatoes
touching all the senses
it is the difference between night and day
complete envy

the love of all things
the connection
the understanding of the limitless
it is sweet potatoes and strawberries
stevie wonder

encompassing the emotion and the
absorption of energy
it is black matter

humility
shangri-la

it is the story
of what it all boils down to

the justification
the truth
the means

it is euphoria
it is sankofa
with atlantic waters for tears

the raiser of african consciousness
mature
the seeing to it
it is jon lucien and
sekou sundiata
ancestrally guided
it is an endless prayer

it is less about love
and more about the continuum

the role of men
the role of women

it is the tool
the incarnation
the purpose

the ritual
the last thing that it is
is purely sexual

it is forgiving
worn like leather
it is the story
comfortably smooth
consistently unchanging

the kiss
the remembrance
the smile
the soul
the magical embrace of
eternity's flame
of fire and ice
they are one and the same

it is the heart
the holding
the rainbow after the storm
the shelter
the dying
the healing
the struggle
the passion
the struggle
the pain
the want to
in the balance
in the pain
it is the ear of the outspoken
the can't live without you

it is a level of being
a field for flowers

a there in the hereafter
a now in forever
a presence of before

this is what we call black love

a poem for jb

think revolutionary on the mic
with tag lines
reflective of black pride
grooving on the turntables
discos and radios
inspiring black folks of the world
to say
i'm black
and i'm proud!

you could feel
the godfather of soul
bringing black back
to the consciousness of
playgrounds and school yards
swaying to the music of
his vision for tomorrow
painted red, black and green
with dashikis and afro pics on the scene
birthing a soul generation
in the midst of race and civil wars
and wars abroad
he said it loud
with feeling
he sang it clear
without fear
sliding across the stage when he had to
falling to his knees so that we
could all have a get back
a take back
on the good foot with our hot pants
saying it loud
oh yeah!

he gave us the feeling
please, please, please
flooding the air ways
cool so very cool
while we marched in the heat and
prayed in the streets and listened
to his funky beat
acting affirmatively
like loving machines
doing it
grooving it you know
like lynn collins
thinking you'd better
get in or be out
of a movement
a love song
that ministered to
the souls of black people

think musical genius
think pride generator
think hit maker
think groove shaker
think mind changer
when you think james brown
with his mic
his cape
his moves
splitting the paradigm of human kind wide open
so that we could all
get up ah, get on up[1]
get up ah, get on up
get on up, get on up

_____

1. James Brown, "Get Up (I Feel Like Being a) Sex Machine,"
   King Records, 1970.

18

Girl

Out-sharpening my enemies
With what Eve knew in Adam

Because I am a girl

I open and close my legs
On the faith that
The good will come and
The toxic release of traitors will run
Like thieves from territories destined
For greatness
Saving virgins from knives
Erected beauty
Slashing at the real war
The core of male identity
My masculine side strikes back
Whipping fights to feel
With the right to dance, rejoice and deal
With the heat of
My will to survive
Mutilated in body but not in mind

Because I am a girl

Without a place for peace
Without silver for pleasure
He burned
My face
My legs
My back
My treasure
For dowries greater than
The hellish skin

I grew out of when charred memories colored my lips
Like apartheid's cancer
With head wraps for cover
Because I am pretty on the inside
"and from his fire, I shall take some of my own"[2]

Because I am a girl

Called
Queen
Bitch
Mother
Fem
Ho
Princess
Dyke
Baby mom
Concubine
Yemeya
Daughter
Wench
Wife
Slut
Lesbo
Geisha

No more name calling
No more hanging from hairs, tongues and feet
Because of annoying husbands
Daring to challenge
The word that was
With God
That lives within me

---

2. Phillippa "Emmannuelle" Duncan, 1973-2003, author of *An Evolution in Reinvention* and *A Work Made for Hire.*

Call me
Heaven on earth

Because I am a girl

Suicide has always been considered
Because the blues birthed rubies in my veins
Swirling and nodding with
The ecstasy of numbness
Because of boyfriends who rape dates
Because they are boys
With sick minds projecting loose cannons
Because they are boys who sleep with boys who sleep
With girls who can keep a secret
So I can catch AIDS and die
Because they are boys who sleep
With boys who sleep with girls
That lie and I tell you this

Because I am a girl

A drunken man
Tossed his 10-month old baby girl
Out a window in Shanghai
She survived eight stories
Slowed by tree branches
Landing in soft soil and
Into the arms of this poem
Breaking only her leg and
I tell you this

Because I am a girl

A woman in Florida

Raped and robbed by men
Then made to have sex with
Her minor son in front of them
And her children
I weep and we all lose and I tell you this

Because I am a girl

I get cut to give birth
I give birth to get cut
I bleed for seven days and still don't die
Says Emmannuelle
Rising on the wings of angels with locs,
Blonde hair, weaves and braids
Espousing the truth poetic
Like Isis in she tongue
And I tell you this

Because I am a girl

I get to choose life or not
Because the condom broke
Or you choked on the responsibility
Of not truly asking for what you wanted
But didn't really want
So I get to wrap it, foam it, coil it, pill it, implant it,
swallow it
Just so you don't have to choose
Other than me
Because I think I love you

I raise our children
Because I think I love you

I don't think

Because I am the esteemed symbol of the universe
Designated to show up/always

Because I am a girl

I work harder
So you can fly when you kiss me
Rub my own back when you diss me
Wipe my value when you spit at me
Put my makeup on when you reject me
Lie about me and speak ill of me
Roll over on top of me
Walk two steps behind thee
Ride shotgun for you
Take raps for you
Wear long dresses for you
Fight by your side
Take your side
Because I think I have to

Crying out for my Country
My Africa
My America
My Pakistan
My Afghanistan
My China
My Harlem
My man
My man
My man

Because I think I need you
Because I think I need cover
Because I think I need rest because I think
I need to think this

Because I am a girl

I now reclaim
My right
To be
To decide
To think
To choose
I now reclaim
My right
To be
To decide
To think
To choose

The toxic release of traitors
Running like thieves
From territories
Destined for greatness

Out-sharpening my enemies
Out-sharpening my enemies
With what Eve knew in Adam
And I tell you this

Because I am a girl

Secrets

I keep secrets
Under the Atlantic's floor
Through the Euphrates River
The fires of Watts and
The endless chatter of Birmingham
Permanently etched in love
The science of synergy
The mathematics of trees
Nourishing the root of
Complexity

I keep them
Under my skin
With deep pockets of trust and
Deposits on receipts, paper napkins and journals
Eyes that hold many
Hands that have felt them
Gripped them
Caressed them
Torn at them
Lips that have crossed
My heart vowing to die for them

I keep secrets
Entrusted like God
Simultaneously releasing their toxins
With the resolve to come clean

I keep secrets
In my walls
Oh, the stories of love
And lies she tells

The miracle of birth
That needed indiscretion
Even his shortcomings
Come through
In cycles of what
I can no longer hold onto

Preserving a basis for freedom
The ability to live again
Hoping secrets
Won't spill from my eyes or
Leak from my vagina
Sweat through my pores
Or revel in liquor induced moments of betrayal
For once they are known
My bare nakedness will
Inhabit the earth
And leaves will reveal themselves
As my covering
But my truth
Will let them
Burn

Remember Me

don't forget about me baby
don't you run off and forget about me

want you to feel free
want you to remember me
when you walk 'round feeling free
got some stories in
my boots

keep them home fires burning baby
keep the syrup hot
and them cakes tasty too
i said
keep them fires burning baby
the syrup hot
and them cakes tasty too
i'll be coming back to you
making my way
with them stories in my boots

want you to feel free
want you to remember me
when you walk 'round feeling free
say a prayer for me
and the souls
in my boots

when i come home
i think i'll take you dancing
take you for a ride in my car
said i'll take you dancing
pretty missy
and take you for a ride in my car

i think i will
once i take off these boots

so don't forget about me baby
don't you run off and forget about me
i'm a soldier for you 'cause
i want you to feel free
want you to remember
when you walk 'round feeling free
that there's muddy waters
on these here boots

so don't you forget about me baby
don't you go running off with some other baby
i got everything you need honey
so go on and set your watch for half past two
'cause soon i'll be walking
the lover man walk
got something sweet for you
and you won't have to worry no more
'bout your baby and
no damn boots

wanna undo what's been done
with my mental guns
firing words of mercy
peace and grace
scrawled in pen
all over my face
'cause when i return
i've got some stories
i want you to see
stories you ain't heard 'bout
what i've seen

Girl Blues
for Milicent Gaita and the girls of the Girl Child Network Worldwide

The rhythm of her body in
Tune with her ancestors
Stopping to rest in the shade along the mountainside
Her sharpness vivid against the sky
Oh! What beauty the morning brings!

Her pain is gone
Lifted by her dreams
She rises

She wanted to give her flowers
Protea for her beloved
A symbol of diversity and courage
Transformed with kisses
Stained lavender 'n wrapped
In mud cloth with scented note on burlap
Inscribed "girl, my love is boundless, it knows
everything"

Some think it was the rapists
The four cowards that took her
The first time because she is a girl
The second because she loved one

She hated them for stealing her butterflies
The long short of her hair
The round flat of her behind
The absoluteness of her blood
This acceptable gender genocide

But the pain had receded
Out of her mind
And back into the land

Blown to bits by touch
Replaced with a prayer
"Oh heaven, I only want to love,
Please give me courage"
And the pain
Transformed like oz
Into undeniable
Beautiful love

Absent hand holding
Shopping for groceries
Hugs at cinemas
Photographs in the park
Not like other gals doing it
With their curious boyfriends
In the dark

She a secret love song rising
In a scat for her life
A blues for girls
For soil loving maidens
Imprisoned by minds
Without souls or butterflies

Free to speak
Because she gave me this...

A voice for gals with limited choices
A blues for Protea
And daughters that swim with sharks

Stopping to rest along the mountainside
For gulps of morning beauty!
Oh! What joy the morning brings!
The pain is gone!

Because she gave me a voice
Beginning with her cry
A blues for Protea
And her sweet, beautiful butterfly

Acknowledgments

"Secrets," written by Tantra-zawadi appeared on the spoken word CD *A Woman's Song* by Shanna T. Melton (2009).

"Girl," written by Tantra-zawadi is an excerpt from the stage production of *Girl: A Choreospective* performed on stages from South Africa to New York City — also as a CD single and on Tantra's promotional video with music by Dana Byrd featuring I'serene Oasis on bass. "Girl" also appeared in the publication *Poetry in Purple* as part of Downstate Medical Center's Domestic Violence Awareness Month in October 2009. "Girl" is also part of Tantra's forthcoming CD *Lifewatcher*.

"Remember Me" is an excerpt from Tantra's stage production *Soldier Blues* which premiered at the WOW Theater Cafe in NYC in March 2010 for *A Night of Three God/desses*.

"Third Eye Kisses" appeared on the CDs *Selling My Diamonds* by Precious Gift (2000) and *Urban Avant Garde - Live at the Nuyorican Poet's Café* by Canhead Records (2001).

"Black Love" written and performed by Tantra-zawadi has

been recorded and is part of her forthcoming CD *Lifewatcher* with music by King Tut.

There are so many people that have blessed me with their love, friendship and creative sustenance over the years, and I thank God for them daily. I am grateful for the love of my beautiful family and beloved children Justin Jelani and Chuma Ayodele. None of this would be possible without a talented team whom I deeply love and respect: Deb Williams, Stephanie Griffin, Chuma Whahid Rasul, and Marilyn Hawthorne for her support during the early years; the Badilisha Poetry X-Change Festival, the Montserrat Poetry Festival, and Roxanne Hoffman of Poets Wear Prada for this beautiful chapbook. Love and thanks to all of you and the poetry community for your beautiful energy and inspiration.

See you out there!

Love Power,

About the Author

Tantra-zawadi, an award winning poet/artist/filmmaker from Brooklyn, New York, has performed to standing-room audiences at venues as far away as South Africa, London, Germany and Toronto. She has performed original works in off-Broadway productions including *Soldier Blues*, and her one-woman performance piece, *Girl: A Choreospective*. She is known for being on the cutting edge as an artist regarding issues such as HIV and AIDS awareness. Tantra's poem and video, "Scarlet Waters," was featured on the Product (RED) video wall to raise awareness for HIV/AIDS in Africa and her short documentary, *A Silent Genocide ~ A Brief Insight into HIV/AIDS* edited by Oliver Covrett, takes another look at the personal impact of the disease.

Follow Tantra-zawadi online:

www.tantra-zawadi.com
www.facebook.com/tantrazawadi
www.myspace.com/tantrais
www.youtube.com/tantrazawadi

www.ingramcontent.com/pod-product-compliance
Lightning Source LLC
Chambersburg PA
CBHW061758040426
42447CB00011B/2357